Master
Of Service

Master
Of Service

Master what you Service and
Service what you Master

Norman Lacasse

Library of Congress Control Number: 2010914157
ISBN: Softcover   978-1-4535-8248-0

This book was printed in the United States of America.

To order additional copies of this book, contact:
Xlibris Corporation
1-888-795-4274
www.Xlibris.com
Orders@Xlibris.com
48916

Contents

Dedicated to my family
Maurice, Annette, Denis, Lise.
I have learned so much from each one of you.

Acknowledgments

This book would not have been possible without the guidance of my publisher and their team of experts.

I am so thankful for all the wonderful people I have met through businesses and seminars. Their impact on me is absolutely tremendous. The great works of authors, living or deceased have left such an impression on me.

The team of family, priceless friends and coaches surrounding me have been true blessings.

Each one of you has helped me to become who I am today.

Our First Meeting

"I don't know what your destiny will be, but one thing
I do know: The only ones among you who will be really
happy are those who have sought and found how to
serve."

Schweitzer, Albert

It was near the end of the evening. The ballroom held 163 people,
they were all going on a 4 months cruise, all around the world.

The President of the cruise ship company was finishing his speech
by saying: "Most people invest in real estate, stock market, gold. But
you decided to invest in your life".

It caught my attention. The dinner had been going very well.
All these guests were invited by the cruise ship company to attend
a "Welcome Dinner" held at a refined hotel in the Fort Lauderdale
area.

They flew in from all corners of the world with many suitcases.
They were to attend the sponsored dinner, and stay over for 2 days

at this prestigious location by the intracoastal waterway, then leaving from Port Everglades, Florida, where the finest ship would take them all around the world.

Some were mentioning exotic names of countries in South America, Europe, Africa, Asia. Their Grand Voyage. For some people it was their second, third, forth and fifth "around the world" cruise.

I was curious.

Who were these people? What kind of work were they doing?

After the speech while they were leaving for their sleeping rooms, I kept thanking them for visiting with us. Real nice people.

Some where in their thirties, some were in their fifties, some were in their seventies.

Two to five times around the world? Four months! Who were they?

They kept walking by. Thanking me. Smiling.

The last couple exiting the ballroom was of middle age, gray hair. I could perceive something special about them.

We exchanged few words. They told me they were from the northeast.

"Is it your first trip?" I asked.

"This is our fifth" they said.

I said "You belong to a group of very refined people". I was curious.

Who were these people? What kind of work were they doing?

He said "Yes, we do have something in common." We then introduced ourselves to each other.

We shooked hands. There was something special in their eyes, in their smile.

Something special in their handshake. Life.

I didn't want to ask, but, I was burning inside to find out. I decided to go for it. "May I ask what you do for a living?"

"We are Masters Of Service"

"Could you repeat please?"

"All of us going around the world are Masters Of Service."

I had no idea what he meant. Master of what? Service of what? Never heard that before!

I was confused and curious by his answer.

She was smiling.

He said "You are very professional in what you do. We were both looking at you this evening during the dinner. Your team was looking up to you. We noticed."

"I do appreciate the compliment. It is getting quite late. May I walk you to the elevators where your suite is waiting for you?"

Before pressing the 18th floor button, she said "You asked my husband what kind of work we are doing. Our ship leaves only in 2 days. We would be happy to tell you more in the morning. Why don't we get together for breakfast, let's say at 7.30 A.M.?"

"Yes, I Said without thinking." I know of a very special place by the beach. I'll pick you up at 7 A.M."

At the exact moment the elevator doors were about to close. He said "Soon in the near future, you could be with us. We'll tell you how to become a Master Of Service." The elevator door closed, and went non stop to the 18th floor.

I said to myself, "What have I done? What did I say yes to? Who were they?

What I am going to learn? Why me? Why not? How?

The Breakfast

No man becomes rich

Unless he enriches others.

Andrew Carnegie

I woke up early. Couldn't figure out why they invited me for breakfast. Should I go? Should I call them?.

I decided to go. I had said yes the previous evening. I drove to the hotel, and was 15 minutes early. They were in the lobby waiting for me.

After and exchange of "good mornings" we were on our way to my favorite place. An intimate restaurant located at a private marina.

We sat in the corner, where to the left we could see sailboats and yachts; and to the right we could see the blue ocean. Stunning view.

The server came and took our order.

I decided to break the ice. I said "Why did you asked me to have breakfast with you? I am extremely flattered, but I would like to know why?

"You were so kind with our group last night" she said, "we noticed that every details were cared for, and you took a personal interest in my husband and I, and you asked us what we do for a living. This is why we asked you. We need to share with more people what we know.

To share with them how to make their life easier, better, faster.

The server came with our breakfast order. I asked him to leave a large pot of coffee on the table.

"As I told you yesterday" he said "all of us going on this cruise are Masters Of Service. Some of us are doctors, surgeons, architects, restaurateurs, car dealers, accountants, entertainers, CEO's, electricians, consultants, airplane manufacturers, caterers and so on. My wife and I are contractors. We all share some very specific common traits. It's a unique group.

Most people don't understand that if you keep doing the same thing, the same way, using the same tools, same people, same systems, they will always get the same results.

Many people don't want to listen to us. They want to have fun, they want to have what we have, without doing what it takes to get there.

If they would only listen, study, and follow what we do, they would prosper faster, their life would be much more richer, with more meaning. They would experience true peace and prosperity."

"Please keep on" I said. I readjusted my chair and got closer to the table.

How they explained it

We see things as we are, not as they are.

Leo Rosten

"We would like to share some serious thoughts with you, if you promise us to share them with whoever is ready to listen" she said.

"Agreed" I said.

He leaned forward, looked deeply into my eyes, while I was sipping my coffee and said: "You will become part of our group. To become a MASTER OF SERVICE, you have got to Master what you Service, and Service what you Master".

I was stunned! I put my coffee cup on the table.

I couldn't speak. My mouth was opened.

My ears and my heart were ready to listen.

She asked the server, to leave another pot of coffee on the table.

"Please keep on" I said. "May I take some notes?" I asked. "I don't want to miss a thing". "I always carry a pen and note pad on me."

She was smiling, and so was he. They knew I was ready!

He asked me "Do you know the definition of MASTER?"

She said "Do you know the definition of SERVICE?"

"Well, I think the definition of MASTER is to excel, and the definition of SERVICE is to deliver something to a customer."

He said: "Yes, it is to excel, to have entire self control, to gain command of, to become an adept in, to be skillful, someone resolved to be an authority, specialized knowledge. The novelist James Michener wrote "The MASTER in the art of living makes little distinction between his work and play, his labor and his leisure, his mind and his body, his information and his recreation, his love and his religion. He hardly know which is which. He simply pursues his vision of excellence at whatever he does, leaving others to decide whether he is working or playing. To him he's always doing both."

I took a deep breath.

She followed with "SERVICE" is an act or a variety of work done for others. Assistance, help. How well someone or an organization is constantly meet the needs of their customers. How people perceive that someone or an organization has met their needs. The ability to provide a service or product in the way that is has been promised. Treating others as you would like to be treated yourself. A contact between an individual or a company that causes a positive perception by a customer. Feeling that a product or service has met the customer's expectations.

Contribution to the welfare of others. The performance of labor for the benefit of others. These are the basic meanings of Service."

"You see, the real magic is when you combine the meanings of MASTER and the meanings of SERVICE" he said.

She added "Start to MASTER every detail you do, then start to SERVICE everything you MASTER." Your life will be changed. The lives of our friends going on this cruise did too. You too can become a Master Of Service. Service what you Master and Master what you Service."

I picked up the breakfast bill, and said "It's on me. I want to know more. Let's take a walk, let me show you the Pier in Dania."

The Dania Pier was stretching far into the Atlantic Ocean. We could hear the waves crashing on the beach, the sound was "Grand" and the view was unbelievable.

We watched as few mega yachts were approaching the entrance of Port Everglades. The breeze was warm.

On the Pier, few people were walking, others were fishing, others were admiring the vast ocean.

"Are you always traveling with this group of people" I said.

"Most of the time. Sometimes they are short trips, and at times they are longer. You have to remember that THE GROUP BUILDS THE GROUP. Like any organizations, each member is building the other members. If you join a group of gardeners, soon you will be growing something. If you join a sports team, soon you will be involved in sports. If you join a group of actors, soon you will find yourself acting some parts in a theater or movie. If you join a group of dancers, it won't be long before you learn new steps. Being a member of the MASTER OF SERVICE group, greatly helps. To be more, achieve more and enjoy more. We learn from each other, and support, and encourage each other by sharing our experiences. It is why it is a necessity to read books, listen to CD's, attend meetings related to what you want to do. You learn from the experience of others, you save time." Yes; THE GROUP BUILDS THE GROUP".

Jet skis were approaching the Pier. Several of them. What a gorgeous morning. People on these jet skis were laughing. They had fun.

"You see these people, they have fun while learning from each other on how to ride these machines" she said.

I was starting to understand more and more.

It made sense.

"Would you like me to drop you at your hotel now or later?" I asked. Secretly hoping that they would have more time to spend with me, so I could learn more from them.

"No" she said. We are free, the ship leaves tomorrow.

"Listen, I have these 2 days off also. I would sincerely love to show you around some real nice places around here.

They said they would like that too.

The Service

"To know even one life has breathed easier because you
lived—this is to have succeeded"

Ralph Waldo Emerson

We sat down on a bench. The pelicans were looking at us like we were
taking over their territory. Huge birds. It was a beauty seeing them as
they came down and landed on the pier and how they were able to
spread their large wings and were able to take off like it was nothing.

"A MASTER OF SERVICE" is just like that" he said. "Everything
they do seems effortless, it seems that they are at ease in what they
do. Have you ever seen professional skating? Have you ever attended
a concert? Have you ever seen an award winning movie? Have you
ever seen a plane landing?

These people MASTER everything they do and SERVICE
everything they MASTER.

Many are MASTERS, but do not service at all what they do. Many
have the SERVICE, but they really don't quite MASTER what they
do. You surely know people like that.

You can see it best in different businesses when they call a department "customer service".

For many of them it should be renamed "Customer Processing"

I laughed and said "I was processed many times. Let me tell you! I can remember many times when someone was telling me; Name? Date of Birth? Invoice number? Debit? Credit? Sign here. Without even looking at me. Without even thanking me.

"When people start taking a deep and sincere interest in other people, business will increase. We are all in the "People Business", selling ourselves and what we do, instead of being in the business of products or services. It is all about people" he said.

She added "Have you ever asked yourself why in a 100 miles radius where there might be 2 or more people doing the same type of work, that one of them is always more successful? One works hard and gets all the rewards while others are working harder and always gets the second place. They all basically serve the same product or service. One of them is a MASTER OF SERVICE, they Master what they Service and Service what they master.

I told them about my dry cleaner. The moment I am in front of her store, she always welcome me by name. She seems to drop everything just for me. She has a smile the size of Texas. She cares for me. She said her business is booming. She is a Master of Service. She is not just taking care of my dry cleaning, she is taking care of me.

"That's what people want" she said.

"When someone decide to become MASTER OF SERVICE, people refer to them as the Greats of the Greats. In any walk of life, they are the Greats, or are on their way to become the Greats." he added.

"Becoming a MASTER OF SERVICE is an art" she said. For 95 % of the people at work, when someone enters their radar zone, they will react according to basically what they have to do: Their job. For 5% of the people, it is about what they can do when they enter the radar zone of another person. They asked how they can be of service to them. To summarize, only 5 % of the people know that for 95 % of the people, it is all about them" she said.

I looked at them directly into their eyes and said: "Got it!"

"A lot of people will tell you they have 5 years, 10 years or more of experience. Most of them have been repeating the first year, every year. Nothing more, nothing less.

Michael Angelo said he knew that the statue of David was in the block in front him. He knew that he had to chisel away what was not David.

People have to decide what they need to "chisel away" from them, to become Master Of Service" she said.

She looked directly into my eyes. She could have touched my soul. She said "It is not how many hours you work each day, it is how much you put in each hour. That's why people earn $ 7.00 per hour and some earn $ 25,000 for 1 hour of their time. What are you putting in one hour? How many people are you touching? How much value are you adding? How many tools do you have working for you?"

He added "It takes discipline to win. It takes time to build value, it takes effort to build it. It is the daily discipline that will produce the results you want. Most people won't pay that price. They want immediate results, without discipline, commitment and plans. You don't build a wall in one shot. Patience does not have too much meaning today. The want it NOW, NOW, NOW. To get there it has to be one step at a time. In the right direction. As slow or as fast as you want.

You need to make a decision. You need to have a plan to become a Master Of Service.

With discipline, you win. Period!"

I took a deep breath. A deep one.

Customer Experience

"We were not sent into this world to do anything into
which we can not put our heart"

Ruskin, John

Their down to earth explanations of what makes a Master Of Service
was incredible. It is like we did know each other for many years.

They made me understand to never pay twice for the same
lesson.

I will always remember a high profile CEO of an hospital giving
a presentation in front of 300 people. While people were checking
in for the function, 2 large blue balloons were bouncing back and
forth in the air. The participants were pushing them back higher and
higher. From the left to the right, from the back to the front. When
the CEO went on stage, her first words were" "Is that what we do with
our patients? Having them bounce around like someone else will take
care of them. None of you did grab the balloon for 5 minutes. It did
opened up their eyes. This is what most people do. Well, the other
guy will take care of it. Let me push this on someone else. I realize
that Masters Of Services grab the ball and run with it.

Most people want to go through a lengthy list of procedures before they start talking with you. It is customer processing, not customer service. You have got to change your way of thinking if you want to achieve different results. People are being sick of being sick and tired. They need you. They need your example as a Master Of Service. They want to see new possibilities. They want someone who will help them break the ice for them, and with them.

Customer service is long time gone. Customer experience is what's needed today.

As a Master Of Service, you automatically eliminate all the amateurs.

You will own the world in the palm of your hands by Mastering what you Service, and Servicing what you are Mastering.

It is about serving people who bring you the money for your services and products. People will always avoid places where no one makes them feel good, special, important. They don't like mechanical process.

People will always notice when there are efforts made for them. They are asking themselves "Do they really want to take care of me? Do they make me shine? Do they care about how I feel? Do they really want to improve my situation?"

The only thing that matter is what "They" want. They are interested in themselves.

They want the "Gold Platter Service".

Everyone of them wants to hear that they are part of "Few Select People". Help them shine, help them feel better, superior.

Ask them how they managed to be such "Top Performers?"

They will tell you.

As a Master Of Service, one of your role is to control the focus of others. And one of them is to give "Priority Service".

People don't mind change. They just don't want to be changed. Make it easy for them to do business with you.

Mediocrity will always be the results of people doing the same procedures, the same way, with the same tools, and expecting new results.

Ask yourself why are so many products renamed as "New" and "New and Improved". This is what people want. Become their partner. Feed their self image. The effect will automatically take care of itself.

This is when the dancer becomes the dance and the dance becomes the dancer.

Companies don't succeed. People do.

Be unique in the way you do things, because the opposite of an artist is just imitation.

The 4 Stages Of Life

"What we need is more people who specialize in the impossible"

Roethke, Theodore

I decided to show them around. We headed south for a lunch in South Beach.

The streets were packed, people from all ages, were walking on the sidewalks.

We found a lovely restaurant with the perfect table overlooking the excitement in front of our eyes.

During lunch, they asked me "Do you know what are the 4 stages of life?"

"Well; growing up, adolescence, maturity, retirement."

"Yes. But there are 4 stages that MASTERS OF SERVICE know about. These stages are

Building

Managing

Blaming

Defending

Which stage are you in?"

I frozed.

No one has ever asked me this powerful question.

The moment you start to concentrate on the "Building" part of anything, and "Building" what you manage; your team, your products, your systems, you are on your way to become a MASTER. Too many people concentrate on the last 2 stages of life. (Blaming and Defending) This is where stagnation takes place. This is where no progress is ever made. As a MASTER OF SERVICE you have to consistently concentrate on BUILDING. This is where the Gold medals are won. That's what creates applauses, that's what create excellence in every spin.

The world has a very limited supply of MASTERS OF SERVICE, there is plenty of room for many. A very limited supply of people who understand the finesse of every step taken.

I could hardly eat my food. It was profound.

"The price of being a MASTER OF SERVICE was the same 20 years ago and it will be the same 20 years from now. A direction is always needed. This is what distinguishes the MASTERS from the amateurs. Each field has only a handful of superstars because as someone said "The Champions have learned to move from the Competition to the Creation". Building, building, building.

"The Masters will always sell you on the feelings you will have, because this is when and where the action takes place". President Kennedy made a decision to send a man on the moon. We were sold on the feelings of pride, victory and being "The First".

"Masters of Service" consistently ask themselves, how can I improve the quality and quantity of service I provide for people? Greatness always starts from a commitment and immediately backed by a plan with distinctive quality of Service.

This was deep!

I told them to slow down a little. Their thinking and their way of sharing all of this unbelievable information was just like a laser. To the point!

"In any area of life, people will judge your performances on what you do for them. And people who are high performers are surrounded with people who are also high performers! You have to give people the best of SERVICE and MASTER that service, so it gives them no reason to look anywhere else.

Build in order to deliver superior quality of SERVICE. Make it your trademark.

MASTERS OF SERVICE are all about results, they make their own rules. They do understand that their Grand performances comes from enjoyment.

Greatness is determined by SERVICE.

Your only job is to create and provide superior benefits to people. They will always buy what you, your product, services, can do for them.

Some people says that life is like a bicycle with gears that we never use. By using and learning how to apply these extra gears will you be equipped to reach new heights.

The moment you are putting consistent effort toward becoming a MASTER OF SERVICE, be sure to know that you are becoming part of an elite group. You will grow into it, it will become your identity. You will know why in every organization, only a small percentage of people achieve Greatness.

The hardest thing to do in a new venture, new business, is to build momentum. You are the one who is going to make it happen. You will understand that customers are at the center of any organization. And this organization of talents and resources is there to provide SERVICE for them.

MASTERS OF SERVICE are working at doing what the rest of society wouldn't try to do. They break the walls of conformity. They improve the parts of a system. They understand that successful people make successful business, not the other way around.

In any field, MASTERS OF SERVICE are listened to, as if they were the "Specialist of Specialists".

The ideal life must include a steel like commitment to serving others. Period!

MASTERS OF SERVICE, concentrate on how they can make money for others, concentrate on how others can benefit from their organized knowledge. Everything they do, gets them closer to where they want to be. They want to include others, because they understand that when the tide rises, all boats are rising also.

Great people plus great systems will always provide extraordinary results. It is not about being active, it is about being productive.

MASTERS OF SERVICE will always see discipline as the power necessary for performance, while the rest of the people will always see it as plain painful. You become a MASTER the moment you make the difficulty look easy. Results are never based on potential, but they are based on Performances.

You are either on the way, or in the way. Leave your comfort zone. You will move from existing to living.

Most people just want to have fun.

Keep building, building, building.

Let others do the Blaming and Defending.

Their Story

"Life is a promise: fulfill it"

Mother Theresa

A little while after lunch, we drove to Key Biscayne. What a scenery, the breeze, the view. We parked the car right in front of the ocean. There it was. The Atlantic ocean with her turquoise water. Couple of people were sailing. We sat down and enjoyed the scenery, trying to absorb it silently. For a while.

"You know" I said, "Everything you have been sharing with me since we met is extremely powerful. I took many notes".

"You were right to do so. Since a long time ago we always take notes also. Sometimes it is not what you hear, but it is what it makes you think about, that you need to write down. Someone can give you the spark for an idea".

"At lunch you kept saying to build, build, build. But who takes care of the daily stuff that needs to be done?"

"Remember: Concentrated periods of building, is going to make a difference in everything you do. It is a matter of setting priorities. If there are small things not done at the end of your list, remember that the dust protects the furniture!"

I had never heard it that way before. It made sense.

After reflecting for a little while I said "I have met MASTERS OF SERVICE before. My uncle is a professional photograph in Montreal, Canada. He has an incredible touch with people beside being great at what he does. Last time I spoke with him, he was telling me that some of his customers travel across the city to have a passport picture taken by him. Pretty impressive."

"You are right, he his a MASTER OF SERVICE" he does something special for his clients, something personnel, he probably ask himself the right questions, empowering questions all the time. How can I do more for my clients? No wonder, people pick up on this, they will travel through a city to get their picture taken. Even if it could have been done at the store at the corner of the street. I am sure he adds value to what he does."

"Last summer I was visiting my family. We went to a little place where they were selling the best French fries. It was a difficult place to find. To my surprise, I met people who drove for more than 1 hour to get their fries at that place. The fries were great.

A French fries stand. But the owner was outside welcoming his clients. He called them by their names. He learned immediately the names of any new customer, an shooked their hands! I went there at 3 different occasions during my vacation. Everytime it was like a big family reunion. He cared for his customers, he added value for them". They felt it, they drove several miles for it, they needed it."

"You see, this guy does what he loves, he puts people first, he manages his activities. By training his team to do the same, providing them with the right tools, and multiplying his basic system, opening new stores, and keeping on building, building and building, he could have an empire." You could apply the same principles in any businesses."

"Is it what you did?"

"Exactly. We started many years ago up north. From almost nothing but a few goals and a passion for life. We bought a piece of land and felt in love with working with tractors. Bought one, then a truck, then another one and so on. With what we did, we kept adding value for people, new driveway for them, crushed stoned for their parking lot, widening a creek to make a lake in front of their house, enlarging ski slopes, so the ski centers could provide more space for their clients. Building highways, so more people could reach these ski centers. Working on runways at the airports, so more people could fly in. We also worked on golf courses, making them nicer and bigger. Always adding value. Bought houses, fixed them up, repainted them, and added more and more value for their new owners.

We sold lots, so more people could own their house. Digging for their water pipes, so these new owners could have the basic necessities. Delivering them loads of black dirt, so they could have the best looking lawns, and the most spectacular flowers.

We loved everything we did. We provided and added value for people. It was for the love of people and the use of our talents and the talents of our team. For them.

We made a lot of people rich, and many companies. We were consistently building, and building and building.

No one can stay in business for long if they don't enrich people in some way".

"Wow; you did a lot! The people going on the cruise with you probably did apply the same principles that you used?"

"Absolutely. In whatever field you are, you can turn it around and become a MASTER OF SERVICE. At a small level, or large level, it is the same, it is Your choice. It's all about adding value for people and more.

You don't sell just a swimming pool, you sell the beach balls and plastic chairs with it. You don't sell just a new pipe for the sink, you sell an total inspection of all pipes. You don't just sell clothes, you go to their house and show them few handpicked items. Just for them.

You don't just sell cars, you bring 3 different models in their driveway. You don't just sell a hotel room, you give them a complimentary gold fish in a bowl for their stay, and they can name the fish.

You don't just deliver plywood, you take a picture of your client sitting in the driver's seat of the delivery truck. They will show the picture to every one they know.

You don't just sell catering to a corporation, you bring the Executive Chef to their office. You don't just sell a drink as a bartender, you offer to adjust it to their taste.

You don't just sell a large piece of land. You put a pony and a bail of hay on it, just for the kids.

You don't just sell wine by the case. You add the cheese that goes with it.

You don't just sell an island. You add a little shack on it and call it a "retreat".

You don't just sell a picture. You add a choice of frame with it.

You don't just sell a BBQ Grill, you deliver it with an assortment of sauces. You don't just sell a large mirror, you sell it with a state of the art glass cleaner.

"It is all about adding value for people. The moment you stop adding value, people will start fighting for the price."

People want to be part of achieving their own projects. They want to touch the tile that's going down in their living room, they want to taste the food that will be served at their daughter's wedding.

That's one of the reason, some cake companies ask you to "add" an egg to their mix. So you can say to your family and friends "I Baked today".

MASTERS OF SERVICE, do Master what they Service and they do Service what they Master.

The Teacher Will Appear

"Making mistakes simply means you are learning faster"

Agor, Weston H.

I was so surprised to hear their willingness to share these specific subjects with me.

I was asking myself some serious questions. Why me? How?

Then, I got to remember one thing I read a while ago that said "When the student is ready, the teacher will appear". I don't remember who wrote it, but it was my moment. I had been waiting and looking for these answers for quite a while. And here it was. I was invited to listen to the Masters. This was my chance to listen carefully, and to apply this new learning in my life.

I needed new and additional directions.

When they told me that the price of success was the same 20 years ago or 20 years from now" I realized that it was about applying discipline to a successful pattern of daily activities, with the right state of mind, backed by a total commitment.

What they were sharing with me was the real difference between Masters and amateurs. They made me realize that each industry has only a handful of superstars, and I had two of them in front of me. It is true that we are all in the people business first. The majority of people don't know about it. They think it is about product only.

They made me realize that all we got is today only, and may be tomorrow. Why not doing the right thing today? "You will never go wrong doing what is right" they said. "You must be more and give more to get more."

It is about asking the right question. Like "How can I improve the quality of life for people?" One on the rules is to always make the steps you do, better and better. Greatness is born out of commitment. Then you move from being excellent to being distinctive.

You want to differentiate yourself. You want to promote your customers in front of them to others. High performers are friends with other High performers.

As a MASTER OF SERVICE, you have to realize that once your customer receive the best service and the best price, they will have no reason to stop somewhere else. It's not about the price only, it's about the Service around the price.

The Difference

We headed for Coral Gables for espresso and biscotti. We drove through downtown Miami. What a fabulous city. Brickell Avenue was sparkling and shining as usual.

We sat at an elegant terrace covered with multicolored large umbrellas. The smell of the finest coffee was in the air. Charming. They immediately took care of our order. They called it "our selection". How nice. It was delivered with a "savoir faire" that was just impeccable. The team serving us was another example of being MASTER OF SERVICE. They cared about us and what they did.

They made our life better the moment we sat down.

She continued by saying "These people are seen as worry free, we trusted them immediately. This is how you become a trademark in your own business. The trademark in your town, county, state, country. You become the "in demand" person."

"MASTERS OF SERVICE are all about results. Not how many hours they have to work. They make their own rules, their excellence come from their enjoyment. They show their abilities in doing small and great stuff. Greatness is always determined by Service. They know that their job is to provide benefit for others. The law of Success is Service. Power implies Service" he added.

I learned that we can become anything we want. Practice, practice, and practice. Any superstar always do a rehearsal before the show.

I learned that MASTERS OF SERVICE are part of an elite group. There are only so few. They grow into their occupation.

They also made me understand that most people don't know that they already are experts. They already know more about their services and products than others. But most of them feel like they are victims. They feel that they are not good enough, not smart enough. The way you feel is a decision. The rest of your life will be influenced by it.

Masters Of Service enjoy doing things the rest of the population won't even consider trying.

There is an aura around a Master Of Service.

With discipline they achieve great performances, they become Champions in their own profession. They know that they can be mechanics or artistics. The ultimate option is theirs.

They know that they become money magnet the moment they start thinking about how to make money for others. It is a boomerang. You throw it a certain way and it comes back to you.

He looked at me said "You know that everything you think and do is getting you closer or farther to where you want to go or be? You can go anywhere you choose. The majority of people enjoys floating on the ocean, with others, going nowhere. They are just being active, not productive."

They were saying that a goal is a dream, a promise with a deadline. They asked me if I was at a place in my life where I have already achieved it and wanted to maintain the status, or if I was striving for more.

What a shock! Almost dropped my cup of coffee on the table.

They were saying that most people see discipline as something painful, to stay away from. World Class MASTERS OF SERVICE sees it as the power for performance. They told me that one of the secret is to consistently improve the human factor in an organization. And to create opportunities for them.

MASTERS OF SERVICE make the difficult look easy. It is a sign of mastery, of true professionalism in any situation.

Results are always based on performances and not potential.

These were mind blowing words they used.

They had so much power in them.

Will I be able to remember all that?

I suddenly asked myself if I wanted to spend the rest of my life existing instead of living. I knew it was my choice. I knew that I had the ultimate control over my life. I knew that most people give the control to others and once in a while get the steering wheel back for few miles. It leads to disaster, because we all know that anything with 2 heads is a monster.

I suddenly realized that it was not all about my products and services, it was first about my performances.

Most people want the harvest without planting the seed. MASTERS OF SERVICE continually plant seeds. That's why their harvest is so huge.

People don't quite understand that anything that continually takes and never gives out, becomes a symbol of stagnation, death.

The majority don't want to be educated, they just want to have fun.

This is your difference.

Deposits, Deposits, Deposits

The quality of a person's life is in direct proportion to
their commitment to excellence, regardless of their field
of endeavor.

VINCE LOMBARDI

It is about creating feelings for people about what you are offering.
Products or services.

Attach their feelings to everything you do, or everything your product or service does for them. Why do you think they call their yachts "She"? Why do you think they say "She can cross the ocean in just few days? Then, you will understand that everything you see around you is making or made millions of dollars for someone. Create feelings for everything you do.

You will become the most successful if you concentrate on helping people and not just selling them. Look ahead, that's why the windshield of a car is always much larger than the rearview mirror. Look ahead. Create routines daily that will create success daily.

You will always have to increase your knowledge in singing, dancing, surfing, in everything you do, you must, if you want to stay on top. They say that the average person watches over 5 hours of television per day. Here is your leverage. Here is your opportunity to start to differentiate from people. Learn more, and put it into practice more.

I will always remember going to visit my sister up north. We went for refreshments in what seems to be an ordinary place. But to our surprise it was filled with an extraordinary team of people who were absolutely delighted to do anything for us.

One of the bartenders told me that he would fix my refreshment exactly as I want it. And after tasting it, he would adjust it to my taste. Never heard about that!

There was a long line of people waiting for him to make them feel special. No wonder there was a line. Many stores wish they had a line!

They say that what you are looking for is also looking for you. It's only a matter of time before the two find each other. It works with everything. There is a line waiting for you.

You know that with discipline, you will win. The emotional need will always be first. They say that 80% of decision making is about emotions, and 20% of decision making is intellectual.

Listen to the heart first, then the head.

People will always act on emotions. First.

Most of the time guys will buy visuals while most of the time women will buy feelings. And remember, both of them wants to be treated exceptionally.

It is what you do every day, every week, every month that will change the rest of your life, that will change where you are going.

You will make history!

The majority of us were raised by learning to make deposits before learning how to make withdrawals.

They both asked me during the afternoon where I was doing my deposits? And what kind of deposits I was making.

Strange question. I was puzzled.

I asked them to be more precise about the question.

"Everything started to change for us the moment we associated the meaning and the feeling of "deposits" to everything we did.

Some people deposit time and effort in their garden, some people deposit time and effort in their singing. Some people deposit time and efforts in their clients. Some people deposit time and efforts in their dancing. Some people deposit time and efforts in their studies. Some people deposit time and efforts in their cooking. Some people deposit time and efforts in raising their children. Some people see that they are depositing in their credit while they are paying their bills.

It is all a matter of perception. The return on your new way of thinking will start to bring fruit immediately, the moment you start to "deposit" in something.

Many just want to withdraw before depositing.

How many deposits will you make today, next week, next month?

Where these deposits will be? Your clients, your garden, your figure skating, your acting career, your pilot license?

The feelings associated with the word "work" will be eliminated.

Let's start to make some deposits.

Tremendous deposits.

The more deposits you will make today, the better you will start feeling.

It works.

Always ask yourself the right winning questions and you will always get the right winning answers.

How is the person you want to be, would do what you have to do right now. What kind of deposits would they make?"

My brother's house won the "House Of The Year" Award in his town, few years ago, for the tremendous look it had. Flowers everywhere, the lawn trimmed like each piece of grass was individually manicured.

What kind of deposits went into it?

Work or deposits?

My brother was never tired of doing what won him an award.

No one gets tired of making deposits.

Take A Vacation From

"It takes a long time to bring excellence to maturity"

Syrus, Publilius

"Anything that you think is in your way, anything that you think is stopping you or slowing you down, you can overcome.

The secret is: Take a vacation from it.

Masters Of Service have learned how to remove from themselves what is not necessary to become what they wanted to be.

People move away from watching 4 hours of television per day, by taking a vacation from it.

Some people move away from smoking, by just taking a vacation from it. One day, three days, a week, 15 days, one month. Then the habit is gone.

Works like magic! Stopping, quitting an habit is difficult. Taking a vacation from it, seems so much more easier to do.

Subconsciously, you know you can always get back to it. If you choose to.

Experts say that after 21 days, you have created a new habit. After 21 days of "vacationing" away from "it" you will be a new person.

Try it. Do it." They said.

Take a vacation from 4 hours of daily television, take a vacation from smoking, take a vacation from desserts, take a vacation from complaining, take a vacation from the mess on your desk, put it in order.

Problems are only temporary situations. Take a vacation from them. Learn that sometimes you are the patient and sometimes you are the doctor.

Emotions are strong, they give you a good day or a bad day. Take a vacation from some feelings.

Take a vacation from worry, what do you get from it?

Take a vacation from envy, what do you get from it?

Take a vacation from sadness, what do you get from it?

Start with a vacation map, new goals, new direction, a quick escape. Soon a new momentum will take place, and they will say "He or She is unstoppable"

Take a vacation from what's bothering you.

You have got to listen to yourself, you have got to find out what is going on with you. You know when a vacation is necessary.

Listen to yourself. Would you have confidence in your doctor if he was not listening to you?

You want a successful life. It has to be filled with many successful days, many successful hours, many successful actions.

Take a vacation from what is stopping you or slowing you down.

She said "We have friends who own their own airplanes. And isn't strange to see that these million dollars flying machines get totally immobilized on the ground the moment someone places a "chock" (that's what it is called) in front and back of the wheels. Next time you are at the airport look a them. They are placed on the ground by people who work at the airport. They say they don't cost too much. Some have names written on them. What is written on yours?" she said.

I did not have an answer. I realized how small things can stop big things. No matter how small it is, it can stop giants.

He said "the goal is to remove anything that is in the way of what you want to become, small or big, take a vacation from it."

A plumber would say "What is clogging up your drain?"

Same meaning, different words.

There is a better route for you.

Stop holding on to what and where you were.

Stop holding on to where you are at.

Take a vacation from it.

Start holding on to what you will be.

Back In Town

"For a long time it had seemed to me that life was
about to begin—real life. But there was always some
obstacle in the way, something to be gotten through
first, some unfinished business, time still to be served,
a debt to be paid. Then life would begin. At last it
dawned on me that these obstacles were my life"

Alfred D Souza

We decided to drive back to Fort Lauderdale, and we took the scenery road. Buildings after buildings by the beach. Some of them so tall, it is as if they were touching the sky. Absolutely amazing architecture.

I was listening to them. They were saying that all of these started with a vision, a while ago it was only a dream. Some people believe in their dreams, some don't, and they quit.

Back and forth we were talking about different subjects. One of them was time.

I said "Where can people find the time to do what they dream of doing? So many things to do today. How do you manage time?"

Her answer was "It is not about managing your time, it is about managing your activities. There are only 1440 minutes that each one of us have. Take away between 420 and 480 minutes for sleep. That's what you have left to use. You can waste them, or you can deposit them into anything that you want".

Never heard it quite like it before.

They were talking about the fact that people got the way they got, by the knowledge they got. They said if people wanted to improve in any area, they need new knowledge, and they need to apply it.

He said "You really won't be anymore than what you are right now, if you keep doing what you are doing."

My mouth couldn't move. He was right.

The moment of truth came when she said "One of the basic rule to become a MASTER OF SERVICE is to realize that 90% of people will always put more hours to achieve something and that only 10% will put more in each hour. They put more products and services into that one hour. MASTERS OF SERVICE know and understand that they are the President of their own life."

I said "So, if its going to be, it is really up to me".

"Most of the time, big things have small beginnings" she said. "The goal is to better the lives of others, put your eyes on them, think about what you can do for others. People will always buy solutions, not stuff. What makes people tired today is not because of what they have done, it is because of what's left to do".

He added "People are motivated by the thought of losing something, more than they are about gaining something. They have a fear of their own potential, a fear of their own feelings."

"The best way to become great at anything is to seek out someone who is successful at what you want to do, study them, do what they do, then you will have what they have.

It is not about falling in love with what they have, it is about falling in love with the work they do. Become one with the love of work" she said.

I adjusted the air conditioning in the car, to a colder level.

I needed it.

I drove them to the hotel, where they had dinner plans with a very well known CEO of a multinational company, who was also going on the cruise with them.

We made an appointment for the following morning at 8 AM. I was to pick them up. I knew it was going to be the last day with them. Their ship was leaving at 4PM that day.

I drove home, kicked the shoes off and went for a swim at the pool. The water was perfect. From the pool, I was looking at some boats passing by on the canal. It is a canal leading to the ocean. It was very late in the afternoon.

I fixed a quick meal for myself. I had an appetite but no appetite. I was overwhelmed by everything they had shared with me during the day. It was less than 24 hours I had met them. My life was altered by meeting them.

I went to bed early.

At 1AM, I woke up, couldn't sleep anymore, my head was running like crazy. All the stuff they had shared with me, just kept coming back to me.

Building, managing, blaming, defending. The fact that I had to make choices. The fact that they saw everything as deposits. The fact that what they were talking about made so much sense. The fact that they were going around the world the following day, and they decided to spend today with me in South Florida.

I was suddenly in my living room. I walked twice around the coffee table. The wealth of knowledge they had shared with me was incredible.

Hard to believe, hard to digest.

I made myself a salami sandwich, thinking at the same moment that I had to make my life, one success at a time, like I eat a salami, one slice at a time.

I woke up at 5.30AM. No more pillows on the bed, no more sheets on the bed. Everything was on the floor. I don't blame it on the salami sandwich. It was a lot of knowledge to digest.

I felt lucky. Lucky is when you are ready, and the right thing shows up in your life.

It did for me.

Time To Go

"Every exit is an entry somewhere else"

Stoppard, Tom

At 7.45AM, I walked in the lobby of the hotel, and at the same moment, the elevator doors opened and there they were. They introduced me to a couple that was going on the ship with them. He was a very well known heart surgeon with his wife. Nice people. Very nice people.

The surgeon and his wife were going to meet a celebrity chef and his wife for breakfast at the hotel's restaurant. Them too were going on the cruise. I saw him from the corner of my eyes. I recognized him immediately. He has his own TV show. Immediately the thought came in to mind that he is a MASTER OF SERVICE, he is the true definition of it.

We exchanged few words while the valet got the car.

We drove to Lantana, Florida. Which is about 25 minutes north of the hotel. I knew of a tiny restaurant on Ocean Avenue, where everything they do is simple and grand at the same time.

From there we could see mansions on the water with their private beaches. Just like you see in the movies. Except, it was reality.

After ordering our breakfasts, I had few questions for them.

Questions I thought about in the middle of the night.

I asked them if it had been like that for them all of their life.

She answered: "No. It was an evolution. We started with nothing. We made deposits, hired people on our team who also made deposits with us. It was a process. We raised great kids also. It is not all about business. It is about having a balanced life, it's about having a quality of lifestyle".

I asked him if they ever ran out of money. I did not know how he would answer this question.

"Yes we did; but we never ran out of ideas. It is all in the mind. At the end of a year for a MASTER OF SERVICE, it is not about the hourly raise they got, it is about the increase in their net worth.

She said to me "Be careful of where you park you anchor. Around wealth, around success. This is vital to remember. Increase your own standards, your self image will change.

Anchor yourself with champions. Champions like Bob Proctor, Wayne Dyer, Donald Trump, Joe Vitale, John Assaraf, Richard Branson, Joseph Michelli, Loral Langemeier, Cindy Ashton and other greats. You might not meet them today, but buy their book. It is not about the books. But, it is what the information in the book will do for you. Look at a book from Judith Bowman about etiquette, she'll explain in details how can somebody "fit in" in just few steps. Tremendous knowledge is shared in books. Most people stop reading when they finish school. MASTERS OF SERVICE read more books than they read during school".

I asked him which areas of my life I should concentrate on. Because me too, I want to leave my mark.

His answer was: "There are six areas of your life that you have to improve immediately in addition to the Spiritual Goals:

Financial and Wealth goals

Free time goals

Relationships goals

Health and Appearance goals

Personal development goals

Community goals

Something magic is going to happen the moment you work on any of these life improvement areas. The other ones are going to improve immediately.

Where you are today means nothing, compare to where and what you will be tomorrow, next week, next month, next year."

We asked for more coffee.

I pulled in the driveway of the hotel with mixed feelings.

I was blown away by the knowledge I got in just few hours with them, and I was sad to have to say goodbye.

We did say goodbye finally. We exchanged phone numbers, and so on.

She said "It was a great deposit we made in you, use it and share it. Society needs it."

"At the end of life, there are no more minutes left to use. It is too late when you reach that point. Use every one of them to get closer to where you want to be and bring people with you. The minutes are passing by anyway." He said.

We gave each other a hug and a warm handshake.

And I left.

Later on that day, I decided to go take a walk at the State Park in Dania Beach.

This is where I started to write this book. I might have misspelled some words. I am sorry. I needed to share my experience.

It could help you. It did for me.

After writing a couple of pages, I raised my head and saw the biggest ship in the world leaving Port Everglades.

Right there at about 1000 feet from the beach, there it was. It was their ship leaving for around the world.

I am sure, I saw both of them waiving at me from the deck.

Them, the MASTERS OF SERVICE.

MASTER OF SERVICE is the first of a serie of books.

Feel free to share your story. Your story about how you became a MASTER OF SERVICE. It can help someone. Someone needs to hear it. Your story could be part of the next book.

Until we meet.

Norman Lacasse
P.O.Box 550492
Ft Lauderdale,Fl 33355
USA

Disclaimer

This book is designed to provide information about the subject matter covered. It is sold with the understanding that the publisher and author are not engaged in rendering legal or professional services. If legal or other expert assistance is required, the services of a competent professional should be sought.

It is not the purpose of this manual to reprint all the information that is otherwise available to people, but to complement, amplify and supplement other texts.

This book is not a get rich quick scheme. Anyone who decides to succeed must invest a lot of time and effort without any guarantee of success.

Every effort has been made to make this book as complete and accurate as possible. You should use this text as a general guideline.

The purpose of this manual is to educate and entertain. The author and publisher shall have neither liability nor responsibility to any person or entity with respect to any loss or damage caused or alleged to be caused directly or indirectly, by the informations contained in this book.

www.ingramcontent.com/pod-product-compliance
Lightning Source LLC
Chambersburg PA
CBHW021919170526
45157CB00005B/2099